Robin Richmond

Introducing

Michelangelo

Thameside Press

For Saskia with love

Distributed in the United States by
Smart Apple Media
1980 Lookout Drive
North Mankato, MN 56003

Text copyright © Robin Richmond

ISBN 1-931983-43-7

Library of Congress Control Number 2002 141379

Printed by Imago, Singapore

Edited by Marilyn Malin
Designed by Frances McKay

Title page art: *Cartoon for a portrait of Michelangelo,* 1550, by
    Daniele da Volterra.
Contents page art: Detail from the lunette *Azor and Sadoc*
    by Michelangelo, in the Sistine Chapel. Thought to be a
    self-portrait.
Pages 4 and 5: Montage showing details from the Sistine Chapel
    ceiling, Michelangelo's plans for the fortifications of Florence,
    Michelangelo's *David*, and the dome of Saint Peter's cathedral.

Photographic credits

Romano Cagnoni: 21
Nippon Television Network Corporation. Tokyo, Japan: Front and
    back covers, 3, 22, 24/25, 26, 27, 28, 29, 30
Scala: 4, 5, 6, 7, 8, 9, 10, 11, 12, 13, 14, 15, 16, 17, 18, 19, 20, 22 and 23
    (insets), 23
Teylers Museum, Haarlem: Title page
Twentieth Century Fox: 24

The photographic montage using Scala images on pages 4 and 5 is
by Ian Pickard.

Contents

Who was Michelangelo?

Michelangelo was one of the most famous artists that ever lived. Some people think he was also the greatest. That's something you will have to decide.

He was a man who created wonderful art in an exciting moment in history. His strong personality made people either love him or hate him, but his art was so powerful that even his enemies had to admire and respect him. He lived a long, full life and saw many changes take place. His work shows us his inner world of private joys and sorrows and reflects the changing world around him.

Looking at Michelangelo's work helps us appreciate what it was like to be alive more than four hundred years ago. But it also tells us about ourselves. It speaks to us as strongly now as when it was first created, because people are still the same as they ever were. Even though Michelangelo died a very long time ago, we can still look at his work and understand it. But we can increase our enjoyment if we learn something of his life.

Early Life

Michelangelo was the first name of the son born to Lodovico Buonarroti Simoni and Francesca Miniato del Sera on March 6, 1475, in a little town called Caprese, in the region of Tuscany, near Florence. Michelangelo's mother was very young and delicate. She found it hard to look after two small, demanding boys — Michelangelo and his older brother, Lionardo. And Michelangelo's father was a *dolce far niente,* a mild-mannered, good-for-nothing man who lost his job as mayor of Caprese soon after his second son's birth. Life was difficult for the Buonarroti family.

Michelangelo's mother decided to send the baby Michelangelo away to be looked after for a while by a stonecutter's wife. So Michelangelo spent an important part of his babyhood away from his home and his parents.

Michelangelo may have thought of his own mother, whom he hardly knew, when he looked at this painting in Florence of a mother and her child. From *Distribution of the Goods of the Church,* 1425, by Masaccio (1401–1428).

The artist who painted these children is unknown, but they give us an idea of how children dressed in fifteenth-century Florence, when Michelangelo was growing up. They are taken from a larger painting, *Game of Little Owl,* anon.

IL TREBBIO

...ixteenth-century painting of the ...a del Trebbio, one of the homes ...the Medici family, who were very ...uential in Renaissance Florence, ...ere Michelangelo grew up. They ...ported everything from painting to ...lpture, writing, and music.

Young men flocked to the court of Lorenzo de' Medici, who was at the center of Florentine life, in the hope of being accepted into his service. Michelangelo was to be one of them. *Scene of Saint Catherine of Siena,* by Pinturicchio (c. 1454–1513).

There was another side to this arrangement that Michelangelo joked about when he was a famous sculptor later in life. His love for stone, he said, came from the milk of the stonecutter's wife, who had nursed him as a baby. He didn't come from a family of artists and perhaps wondered where he got his talent.

Certainly it was not from his father. Lodovico couldn't concentrate on anything for very long and almost never held a proper job again after he was mayor of Caprese. Poor Francesca had three more sons before she died in 1481, when Michelangelo was just six. Many years later, when Michelangelo was famous, he made great sacrifices to help his brothers and his father. Great fame did not necessarily bring great riches in the sixteenth century — as it seems to do today — but he always managed to send them money.

7

Florence and the Renaissance

The "Catena" map, drawn between 1470 and 1490, shows the improvements the people of Florence carried out in their city, widening the streets and creating impressive public buildings. The Florentines wanted the city itself to be a work of art.

Michelangelo was lucky to grow up in Florence. This elegant city was the artistic center of Europe in the period we now call the Renaissance (which means rebirth and refers to a time, from about 1300 to 1650, when classical thought, art, and writing were being rediscovered).

In the century between 1450 and 1550, Florence was like a volcano, erupting with new ideas and energy. Artists, thinkers, politicians, writers, poets, and scientists met and spoke as equals. They were inspired by the ancient Greek writers, who first laid out the principles of mathematics and philosophy. Men such as Archimedes (c. 287–212 B.C.) and Plato (c. 428–348 B.C.) were their guides.

8

In 1459, Benozzo Gozzoli (c. 1421–97) painted the Medici merchant-princes in all their wealth and influence, in the Medici Palace chapel in Florence. The Medici are depicted as the Kings visiting the Baby Jesus.

While there was still great poverty in Florence, the noble families and merchants became very rich at this time. Florence, situated in the most fertile part of Italy and not far from the sea, had many advantages. Banks in the city, in the center of Europe, lent money far and wide. The city's riches came from agriculture and farming, because the land was so good. Florence was able to trade its local products — fine leathers, silks, herbs and spices, dyes, rice, and vegetables — with the outside world, and so generated wealth. And where there is a lot of wealth, there is usually art, for rich people like to invest their money.

The Artist's Apprenticeship

The Artist's Studio by Poppi, whose real name was Francesco Morandini (1544–79). He was called Il Poppi after the village he came from in Tuscany.

Michelangelo wanted to be an artist. Lodovico, his father, didn't agree. He sent Michelangelo to school at the age of seven, but the headstrong Michelangelo was always sneaking off to draw anything and everything. All he wanted was to be allowed to join a *bottega,* a workshop where a young man could learn the skills of art with a master, or teacher. Finally, when he was thirteen, Michelangelo wore down Lodovico's resistance and was allowed to join the painting workshop of the Ghirlandaio brothers. A disappointed Lodovico signed a contract saying that the young Michelangelo could spend three years in the workshop. Michelangelo would have to obey his masters and do whatever he was told, no matter how boring or stupid. But the *bottega* was a

The Artist's Studio by Giorgio Vasari (1511–74)

During his apprenticeship, Michelangelo learned the technique of fresco painting, which he used later on the Sistine Chapel ceiling.

thrilling place for a young artist. The masters taught everything they knew and everything that they'd learned from their masters. It was like a university of art. Michelangelo's talent soon became obvious to the Ghirlandaio brothers. They were so impressed with him that instead of charging him for lessons, they paid him.

When he was fifteen, Michelangelo broke his contract with the Ghirlandaio brothers. He was probably bored and felt that he'd learned all the secrets of painting. He was also eager to move away from painting to sculpting, where he felt his true talent lay. He told a friend many years later, "I am no painter!" But his magnificent work, especially on the Sistine Chapel ceiling, proves him wrong.

Becoming a Sculptor

Michelangelo wanted to learn sculpture. Renaissance artists admired the art of ancient Greece and Rome, as well as the philosophical ideas of the ancients. The work of the classical Greek sculptors is wonderful and very realistic. Figures bulge with muscle, and their stone flesh looks real enough to feel warm to the touch, though carved from cold marble. Michelangelo liked the way Greek statues seem to burst out of the stone as if they are breaking free of chains.

The only place to study ancient sculpture was in the sculpture garden of the great prince of Florence, Lorenzo de' Medici. An old sculptor, Bertoldo di Giovanni (a pupil of the great sculptor Donatello) was employed by the wealthy prince to look after his collection of precious sculpture, and to teach young artists.

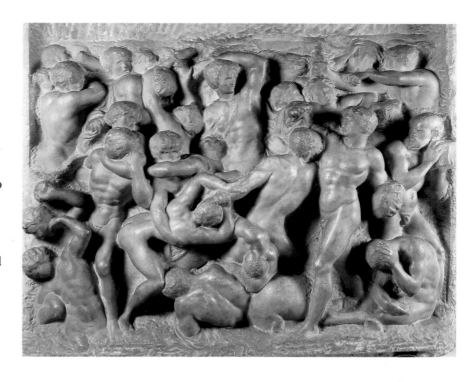

At the age of seventeen, in 1492, Michelangelo sculpted this powerful, twisting battle between the Greeks and the centaurs, legendary animals that were half human and half horse.

There is a story that when Michelangelo was about fifteen, he was copying an ancient sculpture of a faun's head — half man and half animal — in Lorenzo de' Medici's sculpture garden. When Lorenzo saw the work, he commented that the faun's face was old but had all its teeth as if it were young. Michelangelo then made it look as if one of the teeth had fallen out, and Lorenzo was so impressed and amused that Michelangelo became one of his favorites. The faun in this painting may be a copy of Michelangelo's work, which has been lost.
Lorenzo the Magnificent and His Artists by Ottavio Vannini (1585–1643)

Michelangelo was introduced to Lorenzo de' Medici, known as Lorenzo the Magnificent, and immediately charmed the older man. Lorenzo introduced Michelangelo to the great thinkers of the day and encouraged his work. It was a golden period of the young artist's life. Hungry for knowledge, he listened carefully to the prince's every word, and Lorenzo became like a father to him. Michelangelo learned how the rich lived and spent their money, and he realized that all artists need someone to pay for their wares. Lorenzo was Michelangelo's first patron, or employer, and also his beloved friend. Perhaps Lorenzo was the trustworthy father that Lodovico had never been.

Michelangelo's talent for sculpture was soon obvious to all and caused some jealousy. His friend and fellow student Pietro Torrigiano was so jealous that one day he punched Michelangelo in the nose, breaking it and giving poor Michelangelo the prizefighter's nose that makes him so recognizable in his portraits.

Lorenzo de' Medici died in 1492. Michelangelo was sad and gloomy and had little inspiration for his work at that time.

13

Life and Death

What Michelangelo did next may seem strange. He went to the monastery hospital of Santo Spirito in Florence. But he worked there not with the living but with the dead. Like other great artists of the Renaissance, such as Leonardo da Vinci, he cut up and examined dead bodies. He learned all about anatomy, the inner workings of the human body — the muscles,

Scholars are still not sure if Michelangelo carved this crucifix, which dates from 1492. If he did, it was for the prior, the monastic head, of the hospital of Santo Spirito, who had let him study and draw the dead bodies brought to the hospital.

In the left-hand circle in the foreground of this sixteenth-century map of Rome there is a picture of the she-wolf nursing the twins Romulus and Remus, cast out into the wilderness as babies. They were said to have survived through her mothering. According to legend, when they grew up they founded Rome.

The Bearded Captive (opposite) is part of the unfinished sculpture for the tomb of Pope Julius II. Almost every muscle of the body can be seen.

the organs, and the skeleton. This careful study helped him over a bad time in his life. But more than that, it gave him an understanding of the human body in both life and death, and what he learned shows in every piece of work he did after this time.

Sick at heart and bored with Florence, Michelangelo was pleased to be summoned to Rome in 1497. At this time Rome was not the region's main artistic city, but it had something vital for the life of a young ambitious artist. Inside the ancient gates of Rome, there was another city. Vatican City is the center of the Roman Catholic religion, and the pope, its spiritual leader, lives there. Michelangelo knew that one day he would have to go to Rome to work, for the church was very wealthy, and Michelangelo needed rich patrons to pay for his expensive marble.

The Great *Pietàs*

Cardinal Jean Bilhères de Lagraulas wanted Michelangelo to make a statue for a tomb chapel at Saint Peter's, the pope's church in Rome. Michelangelo was delighted with this first important church commission, but unhappy that he had only a year for the job. A statue like the *Pietà* would usually be far too complicated for even the most skillful artist to finish in a year. The *Pietà* (which is Italian for pity) shows the Virgin Mary with the dead Christ lying across her lap. It is a breathtaking piece of work from a young man of twenty-three. The delicacy of the carving makes us forget that we are looking at marble, not cloth. The folds of Mary's cloak seem to weigh nothing. They look as if they could float away in the breeze. Look closely at the Virgin Mary's sash. You can see Michelangelo's signature.

The *Florence Pietà (opposite)* tormented Michelangelo. He worked on it for years (from 1547) but never felt he got it quite right.

When this *Pietà* (the Virgin with the body of Christ after the Crucifixion) was placed in Saint Peter's in Rome, in 1499, nobody believed that an artist as young as Michelangelo could have done it. The story goes that Michelangelo was angry and stole into Saint Peter's in the middle of the night to carve his name into Mary's sash. It is the only work he ever signed.

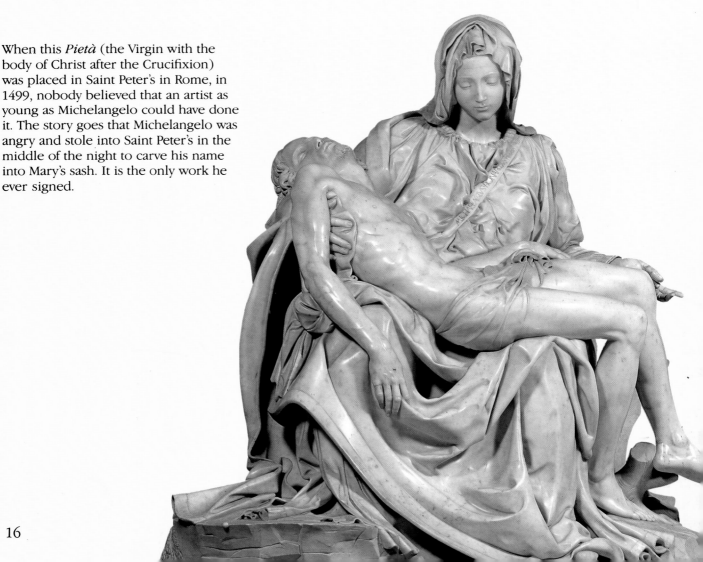

Michelangelo was disappointed with this statue. The marble he used had faults, and he was unhappy with his work on it. He was angry enough to smash Christ's left leg. It's sad not to have it complete, but this burst of temper makes Michelangelo seem very real and human.

In the *Rondanini Pietà,* which he carved later in his life, you can see an even bigger change in Michelangelo's feelings about himself. The figures are much less clear, but there is a terrible feeling of grief and weakness. Michelangelo worked on this last statue for many years. It was never finished. As a tired old man of eighty-eight, he was working on this statue six days before he died. He was an artist to his very last days.

The *Rondanini Pietà (below)*, begun in 1555 and never finished.

It is interesting to compare three different statues that Michelangelo did of the same subject. Artists put their feelings about life into their work, and you can almost read Michelangelo's mind when you study his work carefully.

The first *Pietà* of 1499 is graceful and innocent. Mary and Christ look young, and unscarred by the tragedy of death.

Look at the *Pietà* he began in 1547. This was carved about fifty years later. Here the dead Christ looks old and hurt by his life on earth. The figure carrying Christ to the tomb is Michelangelo himself. You can see the broken nose and the broken spirits of a much older, sadder man.

17

Michelangelo's *David*

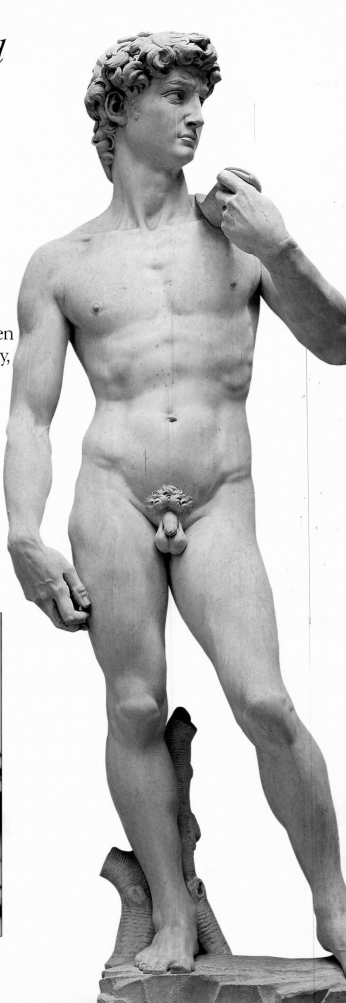

Michelangelo went back to Florence for his next commission, and this was the job that made him really famous. The political leaders of Florence wanted to celebrate the new peace that reigned in the city. They asked Michelangelo to sculpt a statue of David, one of the most famous young heroes of the Bible.

Michelangelo's *David* is nearly fourteen feet high and is now in the city art gallery, though it once graced the main square of Florence. It shows David with his slingshot about to kill the evil giant Goliath. *David* is very much like the ancient Greek statues Michelangelo loved so much in Lorenzo de' Medici's sculpture garden, though much bigger. Look at how Michelangelo has made the head and hands too big for the body.

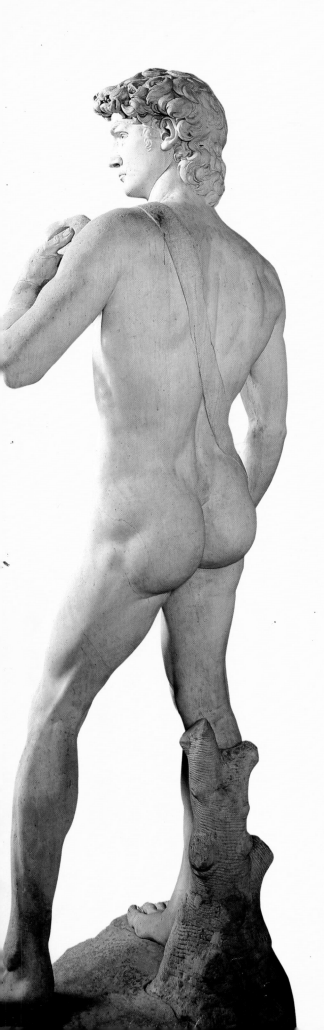

David (1501–1504)
The detail of David's head *(opposite)* shows the furrowed brow and determined expression of the young boy, which were understood by the people of Florence to represent the pride they felt in their great city. The dignity of the statue was a symbol for the dignity of Florence.

This was unlikely to have been a mistake. Michelangelo knew about the human body and its proportions from his studies in the monastery hospital. He probably wants us to remember that the David of the Bible was a young boy, approaching manhood. Boys of that age are often out of proportion, because their bodies are changing very fast.

In 1505, Michelangelo was called back to Rome again. His life was changed forever by this trip. The pope, Julius II, had a plan for the young, ambitious sculptor from Florence. Pope Julius wanted to construct a monument to himself. He wanted a tomb with over forty statues, carved in the very best marble. He wanted it to be as grand as the pyramid tombs of the pharaohs of ancient Egypt.

Rediscovering the Past

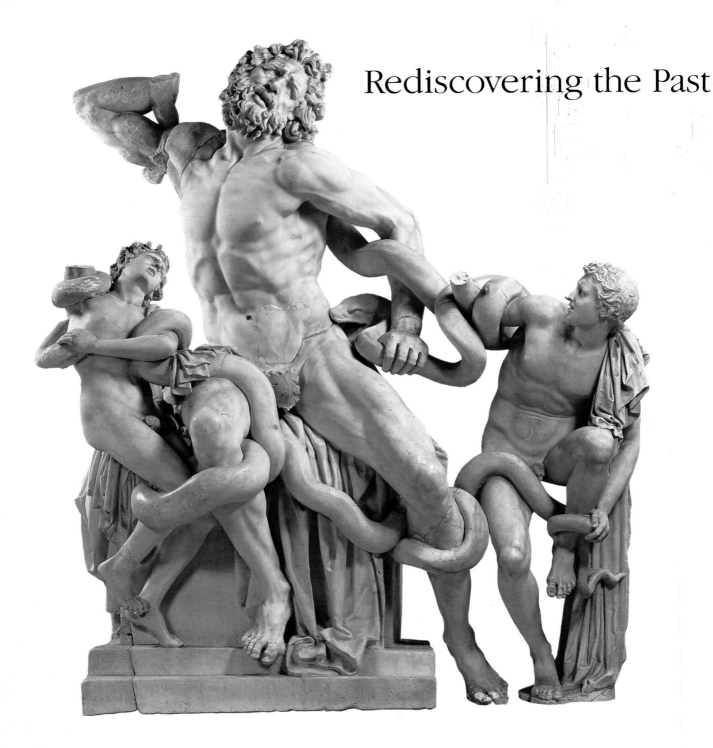

When Michelangelo was in Rome in 1506, he was present at one of the most exciting archaeological discoveries in the history of art. The Roman Empire had once stretched over much of Europe and the East. Roman armies had taken many treasures of Greek art and brought them, and Greek sculptors, back by ship to

In January 1506, a man digging in his vineyard in Rome came across a very large opening in the earth. Hidden in the ground was a famous antique Greek sculpture. It is called *Laocoön,* after a man who was said to have angered the gods. They revenged themselves by sending snakes out of the sea to devour his sons, as the statue shows.

Rome. The classical Greek statues were greatly admired by the Romans, and by Michelangelo. The *David* statue shows this.

In the year 1506, the greatest statue of Rhodes (an island off mainland Greece) was dug up in Rome at the place where the Roman emperor Nero had lived in a splendid palace more than a thousand years before. The *Laocoön,* sculpted by three artists in the first century B.C., inspired Michelangelo, and he declared it a miracle.

Marble cutters have been working for centuries at Carrara in Italy, cutting massive chunks of stone from the mountainside. When he was choosing the stone for Julius II's tomb, Michelangelo lived in this quarry for eight months with nothing but his horse, a couple of workmen, and some food.

Michelangelo versus the Pope

Things weren't going so well in Michelangelo's own work. After all the time he had spent in Carrara happily choosing marble and making drawings, the pope changed his mind about the commission for his tomb. Pope Julius decided that the Church of Saint Peter's needed rebuilding and that the tomb was no longer so important.

Michelangelo was furious. All that work for nothing. During the next forty years, he did receive renewed commissions for the tomb but always for scaled-down versions of his original plan. He never forgot his disappointment. He wasn't a man who forgave easily, and he took his art very seriously.

But this wasn't the end of his

These reconstructions show what the tomb might have looked like at different stages if it had been completed.

Michelangelo's thoughtful self-portrait from the lunette, or semicircular painting, *Azor and Sadoc* in the Sistine Chapel.

A.
The original ambitious plan of 1505

B.
The still huge but slightly toned-down plan of 1513

relationship either with Pope Julius or the Vatican. You could even say that Michelangelo got his revenge on the building that prevented him from working on his great dream of the tomb.

In later life, he became an architect and designed the dome of Saint Peter's, which can be seen from many places throughout Rome. It is part of the Roman skyline. And Michelangelo was to make his mark inside the Vatican as well.

The relationship between Pope Julius and Michelangelo wasn't easy. They were both moody, headstrong men who were used to having their own way. The normally silent corridors of the Vatican rang with their arguments. But though they argued, they respected each other.

This portrait of Pope Julius II was painted in 1512 by another great Renaissance artist, Raphael (1483–1520).

C.
The third plan of 1516

D. The fifth plan of 1542

You can see the number of statues getting smaller and smaller!

The Commission to Paint the Sistine Chapel Ceiling

A reconstruction from the film *The Agony and the Ecstasy* shows what it might have been like to help Michelangelo. The apprentices are suspended on scaffolding high up above the ground. They are helping by mixing colors and washing brushes.

Michelangelo had to obey the pope, and when Julius asked him to repaint the ceiling of the Sistine Chapel in the Vatican, he could hardly refuse. Yet Michelangelo told the pope to choose someone else for the job. The pope, however, paid no attention whatsoever to Michelangelo's protests.

The Sistine Chapel was started by Julius's uncle, Pope Sixtus IV, in 1473. It was a special chapel for prayer but also served as the place where the new popes were elected. Julius thought the decoration of the chapel was too dull. The ceiling had been covered with tiny gold stars on a blue background. Julius wanted figures instead and thought Michelangelo would be good at this. Michelangelo was very upset. He told the pope that he couldn't do the job properly: he was a sculptor, not a painter.

This painting from the Sistine Chapel ceiling tells the Bible story of the Expulsion of Adam and Eve from the Garden of Eden. On the left, Adam and Eve are picking the fruit of knowledge, offered by the serpent-woman. They are happy. On the right, they are being driven out of the Garden because they have broken God's command, and they are ashamed and terrified.

This wasn't actually true. Michelangelo had painted a beautiful picture two years before in Florence, for the Doni family, and had studied the art of painting with the Ghirlandaio brothers as a boy in Florence. He was an excellent painter.

But Michelangelo wanted to get on with the tomb sculpture, and he didn't want the problems of learning how to paint a ceiling that is over sixty feet in the air, the height of a three-story building. He knew it would take years. He knew he'd have difficulty using the special technique employed on walls and ceilings known as fresco painting. He knew that his whole life would be taken over by the Sistine Chapel ceiling — and he was right!

It took him over four years of back-breaking work to complete this gigantic project. He worked alone for most of the time, because he

was too much of a perfectionist to put up with other people's slipshod work. He worked in terrible conditions. In order to paint, he made a special stool that he leaned against and rested his head on. The paint spattered in his face. His back was in agony. He couldn't see properly when he wasn't looking upward. He was lonely and discouraged. His clothes were so filthy that they rotted on his body.

His life was a misery in many ways. Pope Julius nagged him all the time and forgot to pay him. Once Pope Julius even hit Michelangelo with his cane.

But deep in his soul Michelangelo must have loved the work and realized that it was very special. An artist cannot work in the same place on the same thing for such a long time without creating something extraordinary. Today, when

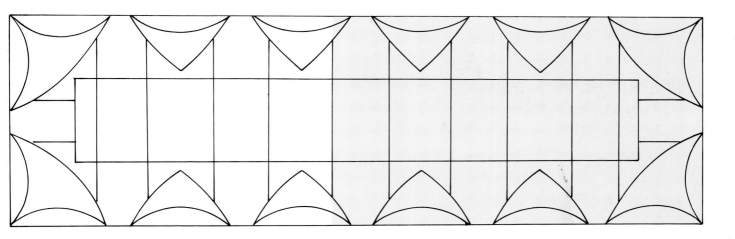

This photograph *(left)* shows the second half of the ceiling. God creates Eve; Adam and Eve are banished from Paradise; God tells Noah to sacrifice his son; God sends the Flood; and Noah is found drunk by his sons.

Lunettes are semicircular paintings. There are fourteen lunettes in the Sistine Chapel. Michelangelo filled them with pictures of the Ancestors of Christ. The two characters below are from the lunette called *Zorobabel, Abiud, and Eliachim*.

The Sistine Chapel ceiling was a very large space for Michelangelo to paint. You can get an idea of how large it is by looking at the photograph on the left. The blue portion of the plan above indicates the part of the ceiling that is shown in the photograph. The ceiling is 132 feet by 46 feet, roughly the size of two and a half tennis courts. Michelangelo painted over 282 figures on the ceiling (not including the lunettes). All of this took him four years and five months, or roughly 1,600 days.

people talk about Michelangelo, they usually mention the Sistine Chapel ceiling first. It is a masterpiece. It shows us the history of the creation of the world through religious stories. But the wonderful thing about it is that you don't have to be of any particular religion to enjoy the painting, because the stories that Michelangelo tells are for everyone. They are about darkness and light, good and evil, creation and destruction.

The Sistine Chapel ceiling is one of the wonders of the world. Photographs don't communicate the power of the painting. It is overwhelming, huge, energetic, brilliant. The three hundred figures seem to spring out of the ceiling with such force that you want to cover your head so they don't come crashing down on you.

Restoring the Ceiling

For the last ten years, a team of dedicated experts has been cleaning centuries of dirt off the ceiling of the Sistine Chapel so that we can admire Michelangelo's original work. They have spent ten years cleaning the masterpiece that took Michelangelo four years to paint, so you can imagine how carefully they have worked.

Slowly and surely, with sponges soaked in a special mixture of chemicals and pure water, they have been taking the darkness away from Michelangelo's painting and revealing his brilliant colors. People who thought of Michelangelo as a gloomy painter who was much too fond of black have had to think again. The restorers have shown us that the black comes off with a careful wipe of the sponge, revealing zingy pinks, lemony greens, and sunflower yellows underneath.

The method Michelangelo used to paint the ceiling is called fresco painting. *Fresco* means fresh in Italian. It is a very difficult technique. Fresco painting is done directly on the wall or

ceiling. The painter must use only special paint made by grinding minerals taken from the earth. The paint is mixed with pure distilled water and painted onto a wet surface that has been carefully and freshly prepared. The surface is made of plaster, which contains lime, and the lime mixes with the water in the paint and so causes a chemical reaction. The paint becomes part of the surface, and the only way to remove it is with a hammer! You can't wipe away fresco with a wet rag. So you see that the restorers of the Sistine Chapel ceiling haven't removed any of Michelangelo's work.

Michelangelo learned a lot about fresco technique as he went along. In some of the first scenes he painted, the paint didn't stick to the ceiling. If the plaster is too wet when the paint is applied, the colors will just drip down the wall in a mess. If the plaster is too dry, the paint won't mix with the lime and it will crack. If the plaster isn't quite right, the paint will grow moldy. Michelangelo had a lot of problems to overcome.

The
Last Years

From 1534 to 1541, Michelangelo returned to the Sistine Chapel to paint the *Last Judgment* on the altar wall. The painting tells us a great deal about the way Michelangelo was feeling toward the end of his life — tired and frustrated. But it is a work of great power.

In 1534, Michelangelo returned once more to the Sistine Chapel. A quarter of a century had passed. The world had changed, and so had Michelangelo. He was no longer young, and he had suffered much loneliness, for he was a man who made few close relationships till late in life.

He was commissioned in 1534 to paint the *Last Judgment* on the end wall of the Sistine Chapel. This work is as gloomy and sad as the Sistine Chapel ceiling is exciting and happy.

It would be too easy, though, to say that the rest of Michelangelo's life was unhappy. Many of his great sculptures come from this time. He painted, designed buildings, and wrote some exquisite poetry. His friendship with the young Roman nobleman Tommaso de' Cavalieri inspired quantities of drawings and poems. His own belief in God grew stronger, especially because of his friendship with the pious noblewoman Vittoria Colonna.

On February 18, 1564, Michelangelo died. He was almost ninety years old, an exceptional age for the time. He was hard at work on a statue.

Some Key Dates

Left events	Year	Age	Right events
	1475	0	Michelangelo Buonarroti born March 6 at Caprese in Tuscany, Italy
Mother dies	1481	6	
	1488	13	Apprenticed to the Ghirlandaio brothers
Leaves Ghirlandaio workshop for Lorenzo de' Medici's service	1490	15	
	1491–92	17	Madonna of the Steps/Battle of the Centaurs
Michelangelo leaves Florence	1494	19	
	1497–99	24	Pietà at Saint Peter's in Rome
David	1501–04	29	
First contract for Julius's tomb	1505	30	
	1506	31	Laocoön discovered in Rome
Michelangelo signs contract to paint Sistine Chapel ceiling	1508	33	
	1513	38	Pope Julius dies
	1513–16	41	Bound Slave sculptures
	1529	54	Michelangelo employed to design fortifications for the city of Florence
Commissioned to paint the Last Judgment. His father dies	1534	59	
Leah/Rachel sculptures for Julius's tomb	1542–45	70	
	1555	80	Begins Rondanini Pietà
Designs model of Saint Peter's dome	1561	86	
	1564	88	February 18, Michelangelo dies

Index

A **bold** number indicates that
the entry is illustrated on that page.
The same page often includes
writing about the entry, too.